★ HOW TO BECOME AN ★

ACCIDENTAL
ACTIVIST

HOW TO BECOME AN

ACCIDENTAL ACTIVIST

Elizabeth MacLeod &
Frieda Wishinsky

illustrated by
Jenn Playford

ORCA BOOK PUBLISHERS

Text copyright © Elizabeth MacLeod and Frieda Wishinsky 2021
Illustrations copyright © Jenn Playford 2021

Published in Canada and the United States in 2021 by Orca Book Publishers.
orcabook.com

Library and Archives Canada Cataloguing in Publication
Title: How to become an accidental activist / Elizabeth MacLeod & Frieda Wishinsky; illustrated by Jenn Playford.
Names: MacLeod, Elizabeth, author. | Wishinsky, Frieda, author. | Playford, Jenn, illustrator.
Description: Includes bibliographical references and index.
Identifiers: Canadiana (print) 2020033722x | Canadiana (ebook) 20200337300
| ISBN 9781459826113 (hardcover) | ISBN 9781459826120 (pdf) | ISBN 9781459826137 (EPUB)
Subjects: LCSH: Political activists—Biography—Juvenile literature. | LCSH: Social reformers—Biography—Juvenile
literature. | LCSH: Social action—Juvenile literature. | LCSH: Political participation—Juvenile literature.
Classification: LCC HN13 .M33 2021 | DDC j361.2092/2—dc23

Library of Congress Control Number: 2020945016

Summary: This nonfiction book for middle-grade readers is full of stories about inspiring activists who have
accidentally changed the world. The activists profiled are a variety of ages and come from around the world.

Orca Book Publishers is committed to reducing the consumption of nonrenewable resources in the making of our
books. We make every effort to use materials that support a sustainable future.

Orca Book Publishers gratefully acknowledges the support for its publishing programs provided by the
following agencies: the Government of Canada, the Canada Council for the Arts and the Province of British
Columbia through the BC Arts Council and the Book Publishing Tax Credit.

Cover and interior illustrations illustrations by Jenn Playford
Edited by Kirstie Hudson

Printed and bound in South Korea.

24 23 22 21 • 1 2 3 4

CONTENTS

INTRODUCTION

How do you become an accidental **activist**—someone who stands up, speaks out and confronts ignorance, cruelty, violence and indifference?

How do you deal with changing the world when so many obstacles stand in your way?

How do you persuade people who resist change?

How do you deal with powerful politicians and leaders?

These are questions all activists face.

And all activists learn that change is hard.

Change takes time, courage, patience, perseverance, flexibility and knowledge.

You can't make change by yourself. You need other people to help you. You need to inspire people to join you.

Change is challenging and frustrating. But change is also important and meaningful.

"Every single day, every single individual—every one of us—can make some kind of impact."

—Jane Goodall, scientist

In this book we explore what makes someone become an activist for positive change, such as equal and just rights for all, clean water and air, or solutions to the climate crisis.

Each person has a different story.

Each person comes from a different background, family, country, religion.

Some activists are women. Some are men.

Some are young and some are old, but each activist shares a common goal.

They want to make the world a better place.

Is there something you'd like to change in the world?

We hope that reading about these amazing activists inspires you to think of ways you can make a positive change in the world.

After all, we're all on this planet together.

We all need each other.

MINERVA HAMILTON HOYT
"APOSTLE OF THE CACTI"

HER TIRELESS EFFORTS TO ESTABLISH JOSHUA
TREE NATIONAL MONUMENT CONTRIBUTED TO
A HEIGHTENED APPRECIATION, NOT ONLY OF
THE JOSHUA TREE, BUT OF THE TOTAL DESERT
ENVIRONMENT.

BILLY HOLCOMB CHAPTER
ANCIENT AND HONORABLE ORDER OF
E CLAMPUS VITUS
OCTOBER 5, 1980

Jacinda
Ardern

WE STAND TOGETHER

Ai Wei Wei

CHAPTER ONE
FIND YOUR PASSION

In 2013 Typhoon Haiyan destroyed Marinel Ubaldo's home in the Philippines and killed more than 6,000 people. Ubaldo, then 16, was determined to tell the world what had happened and how the effects of **climate change** had devastated her family and community. She wanted people in power to act before it was too late.

AHA!

Storm Power

What's the difference between a cyclone and a typhoon? They are both powerful storms, but typhoons occur in the northwest Pacific Ocean, and cyclones hit the southern Pacific and the Indian Ocean.

Now she travels all over the world. She explains how rising seas and warming oceans make typhoons more powerful. She talks about how **fossil fuels** pollute the oceans, forcing fishermen like her father to fish dangerously far out to sea in less polluted waters.

"For me, it's important that people can hear a firsthand story," she said. "If we postpone this and wait for another disaster for us to decide, then maybe we might never see what tomorrow brings. We might lose our future."

Ubaldo's passionate words help people understand what she's experienced and what is at stake if the world does nothing to slow climate change.

Passion is key to changing the world. It's about caring so much that you have to do something. Passion inspires people to work toward change despite resistance and obstacles.

Litia Baleilevuka also speaks passionately about climate change. In 2016, when Baleilevuka was 18 years old, Cyclone Winston hit her community in Fiji. Thousands of people were killed, listed as missing or left homeless. Her mother's village, Nasau on Koro Island, which was once a haven of beauty and peace, was shattered—the cyclone blew houses and people away. Baleilevuka told her story at the **United Nations (UN)** climate talks in Poland in 2018.

Young activists like Ubaldo and Baleilevuka often lead the fight for change. They recognize that their lives will be impacted for years to come unless people act now.

PRESERVING THE BEAUTY OF THE DESERT

Minerva Hamilton Hoyt

(1866–1945)

Today Joshua Tree National Park in southern California is a beloved and protected area. But in the late 1800s, many people didn't appreciate the unique beauty of the desert.

That is, they didn't until the 1890s, when Minerva Hamilton Hoyt came along. Born on a cotton **plantation** in Mississippi, Hoyt later moved to California with her husband. As she traveled west by train, she was awed by the rugged beauty of the desert.

Soon she began riding her horse through the desert and camping with her maid among the cactuses and Joshua trees. When her husband died, visiting the desert comforted her in her grief.

She was determined to protect the land she loved.

Hoyt was wealthy and knew important people. Still, getting politicians and businessmen to support her cause was a challenge. She had to convince them the desert was not a wasteland but a special place.

How do you do that?

Hoyt organized elaborate exhibitions of desert plants in places like New York and London, England. Just as she'd hoped, visitors were amazed and impressed— but she still needed to do more to protect the area now known as Joshua Tree. Hoyt hired Stephen Willard, a famous landscape photographer, to take photos of the desert. She sent two albums of those photos to then president Franklin Roosevelt. Her plan worked.

In 1936 Roosevelt signed Proclamation 2193, establishing Joshua Tree National Monument. In 1994 Joshua Tree became a national park.

Minerva Hamilton Hoyt loved the desert. She wanted to share its beautiful landscape with others and worked tirelessly to make Joshua Tree a national park.

AN ARTIST SPEAKS OUT

Ai Weiwei

(1957–)

There are many ways to protest. Some people speak up. Some people use social media. Some write books and articles. And some, like Ai Weiwei, create art. Ai has combined his eye-catching art with powerful words to stand up to the Chinese government's repression of **free speech** and its disregard for human rights.

Some people have described him as "the most dangerous artist in the world." And if *dangerous* means an artist who is not afraid to speak against a regime that tries to silence people who disagree with its policies, then Ai fits the bill.

As the son of Ai Qing, a prominent Chinese poet who was called an "enemy of the people" for his writing and **exiled** with his family to labor camps in remote parts of China, Ai Weiwei understood how difficult and important it is to stand up to a tyrannical regime.

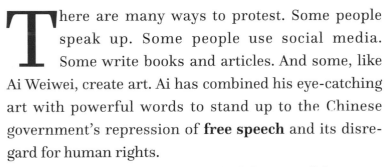

Left: Artist and human rights advocate Ai Weiwei holds up porcelain sunflower seeds—part of his art exhibition. Art is this artist's way of pointing out injustice in his native China and around the world.

TAKE ACTION

ARTISTS TAKE A STAND

In 1937 Pablo Picasso created the painting *Guernica* after the bombing of a small town in Spain that killed hundreds of innocent people, mostly women and children. Other artists, such as Jacob Lawrence, Gordon Parks, Banksy, Dorothea Lange and Norman Rockwell, have portrayed unfairness, injustice and suffering through powerful paintings and photographs.

When Ai was 19 and his family was finally allowed to return from exile, he decided to study art in New York. When his father became ill in 1993, Ai returned to China where he began producing his powerful and controversial art. In 2008 an earthquake hit China's Sichuan Province and thousands of people were killed, some because of poorly built schools. Ai wrote angry blogs and created art about the tragedy. Chinese government officials responded by threatening and beating him, charging him with financial crimes and arresting him. But that didn't silence Ai. Through his powerful photography, film, sculptures and paintings, he has gained support all over the world.

Left: *Ai Weiwei highlights the refugee crisis with an art installation of life vests in Berlin, Germany.*

Ai Weiwei marches with fellow artist Amish Kapoor in support of refugees—people who have been forced to flee their home and country because of political persecution, poverty or famine.

"My wish: use art to turn the world inside out."
—JR, artist

"My favorite word? It's act."
—Ai Weiwei, artist

CARING FOR ALL HER PEOPLE

Jacinda Ardern

(1980–)

> "Unless someone like you cares a whole awful lot, nothing is going to get better. It's not."
>
> —Dr. Seuss, from *The Lorax*

> "Do not think your single vote does not matter much. The rain that refreshes the parched ground is made up of single drops."
>
> —Kate Sheppard, women's rights advocate

Maybe it was spending her first years in Murupara, a tough New Zealand town full of gangs. Maybe it was the influence of her father, a law enforcement officer, and her mother, who worked in a school cafeteria. Maybe it was her optimistic personality, which led her to start a "happy club" when she was a kid. Whatever qualities and experiences led to Jacinda Ardern's remarkable career as the world's youngest female head of state, they shape the way she treats her people, her country and the world.

By the time she was 17, Ardern knew she wanted to help make people's lives better, and she became involved in politics. In 2005 Ardern worked in former British prime minister Tony Blair's cabinet office, helping local communities work with small businesses. At age 28 Ardern became the youngest member of the House of Representatives in New Zealand. In her first speech she said that the Māori language, spoken by the **Indigenous Peoples** of New Zealand, should be taught in schools.

Jacinda Ardern celebrates the Māori contribution to New Zealand in World War II.

After the shootings at two Christchurch mosques, Jacinda Ardern stands up against terror, discrimination and hate.

In 2017 Ardern became prime minister of New Zealand. She immediately pledged that the Māori would be treated fairly. She promised to address climate change. She promised to make things better for young people and help small businesses. She knew the road toward these goals would be hard, but she believed they could be accomplished.

And then, in March 2019, a 28-year-old Australian white supremacist killed 51 people and injured 49 others—men, women and children—in shootings in two mosques in Christchurch. When she heard the news, Ardern didn't hesitate. She showed compassion and support for the Muslim community. She spoke up against extremism and hate. Then she changed the gun laws in her country, banning all assault rifles and military-style semiautomatic weapons. When the coronavirus pandemic hit the world in 2020, Ardern immediately imposed consistent and tough measures to combat the spread of the highly contagious disease the virus caused.

In a clear, caring, science-based way Jacinda Ardern discusses how to address COVID-19, the disease caused by the SARS-CoV-2 virus.

CHAPTER TWO
DON'T ACCEPT THINGS AS THEY ARE

Activists recognize that if someone doesn't stand up, nothing will ever change.

This was true of Marjory Stoneman Douglas, a journalist, environmentalist and women's rights **advocate**. Stoneman learned that the Everglades, a tropical wetland in southern Florida, were vital to the **ecology** of Florida and needed protection. In 1947 she wrote *The Everglades: River of Grass*, which became a bestseller. Despite the popularity of her book, when Stoneman was 79 she discovered that a large part of the Everglades was about to be developed into an airport for jet planes. Stoneman immediately took action. She founded the Friends of the Everglades and the airport was stopped.

Lawton Chiles, Florida governor from 1991 to 1998, said Douglas was "not just a pioneer of the environmental movement, she was a prophet, calling out to us to save the **environment** for our children and our grandchildren."

Douglas was awarded the Presidential Medal of Freedom in 1993. Many places are named after her, including Marjory Stoneman Douglas High School in Parkland, Florida.

That school and its students were victims of a mass shooting in February 2018. Seventeen students and staff were killed. After the horrific event, students at Stoneman Douglas decided to become activists and advocate to change gun laws. They led March for Our Lives rallies that drew millions of people to the cause.

Accidental activists like Marjory Stoneman Douglas and the Parkland students see injustice and do something about it.

It's never easy. Many people stand in the way of change out of fear. Others don't want to lose power. Some do nothing because they think change is too hard, requiring too many sacrifices or too much time and effort. But activists know that what they do brings hope and change to many lives.

FOR THE LOVE OF PEOPLE AND ANIMALS

Jane Goodall
(1934–)

Jane Goodall has always been fascinated with nature. She loved the toy chimpanzee her father gave her when she was a year old. She snuck into the henhouse at her parents' home when she was four to see how chickens laid their eggs. And when she learned to read, she was enchanted by the Dr. Dolittle books and wanted to visit Africa.

It was unusual for girls to study animal behavior in those days, but Goodall's mother encouraged her, saying, "Jane, if you really want something, and if you work hard, take advantage of the opportunities and never give up, you will somehow find your way."

Goodall didn't have the money to attend university to learn about animals. But a friend invited Goodall to her family's farm in Kenya, and there, in 1957, Goodall met the renowned anthropologists and paleontologists Dr. Louis Leakey and Mary Leakey. They were impressed by Goodall's thoughtful approach to science and hired her as their assistant. This experience made her realize she wanted to discover new things about animals through careful, patient observation. "I wanted to come as close to talking to animals as I could," she said. Goodall began to fulfill that dream when she studied wild chimpanzees in western Tanzania, on the eastern shore of Lake Tanganyika.

At first the chimpanzees ran away in fear, but Goodall learned how to interact with them. She proved that chimpanzees are not vegetarians, which most people thought at this time. She also proved that they make tools. Her findings led to an offer to study for a PhD at Cambridge University. She became one of the world's foremost chimpanzee experts. She also wrote books and articles and gave talks all over the world.

Over the years Goodall has established foundations for wildlife research, education and conservation, as well as the Jane Goodall Institute. When she realized that humans were destroying the natural habitat of chimpanzees, she became an activist for preserving natural spaces and the planet.

AHA!

Talking Animals

The Dr. Dolittle stories were first published in 1920 by Hugh Lofting as "story-letters" to his kids while he served in World War I. Lofting's character, Dr. Dolittle, loves animals and learns to speak their language. He takes off for Africa to save dying monkeys.

Top: *Jane Goodall checks out a baboon in Tanzania.*

Bottom: *A chimpanzee mom and baby hang out.*

IT'S OUR FUTURE

Greta Thunberg

(2003–)

Swedish environmental activist Greta Thunberg speaks out at meetings around the world.

Greta Thunberg was nine when she first heard about climate change. That year Sweden was hit by terrible fires. It made Thunberg angry and determined. Why wasn't anyone doing anything to stop it? Why were big fossil fuel companies allowed to destroy the climate? Why weren't politicians and other adults standing up to stop the coming devastation?

Thunberg was diagnosed with **Asperger's syndrome.** She thinks her condition may be partly why she is so focused on one issue. When she was 15, that focus led her to sit in front of the Swedish Parliament and protest for the first time. Within a few months, her protest and words had inspired others to join her and speak up about climate change.

She has organized massive student protests around the world. In March 2019 an estimated 1.4 million students in 110 countries marched out of school to protest climate change.

In Italy, Greta Thunberg calls for action now on climate change.

In August 2019 Thunberg attended climate talks in New York City, sailing across the Atlantic to get there instead of flying. She doesn't believe in flying because the fossil fuels planes burn contribute to climate change. On September 20 that same year, six million students walked out of their classes in a climate strike. They were joined by people of all ages, everyone insisting that the world's leaders do something about climate change.

"If you choose to fail us," said Thunberg, "I say we will never forgive you." She spoke passionately at the UN and joined 14 other young people in lodging a formal complaint stating that the climate crisis endangers lives and that governments' failure to address the crisis violates the UN Convention on the Rights of the Child.

Thunberg believes the time to act is now. "We cannot solve the crisis without treating it as a crisis," she said. "You say you love your children above all else, and yet you're stealing their future in front of their eyes."

Greta Thunberg leads a march in New York City calling for action against climate change. Millions of young people around the world march along with her for our planet and future.

Greta Thunberg holds a sign that reads "School Strike for the Climate" in Swedish.

GOODBYE, PLASTIC

Melati Wijsen
(2001–)

and Isabel Wijsen
(2003–)

BYE BYE
PLASTIC
BAGS

> "You really can change the world if you care enough."
>
> —Marian Wright Edelman, children's advocate

In October 2013 Melati and Isabel Wijsen started an organization called Bye Bye Plastic Bags. Melati was 12 and Isabel was 10. "You see, we didn't want to wait until we were older to make a difference...It was more like, what can we do, as kids, right now," Melati explained.

The girls were inspired as students at Bali's Green School. It's an international school that encourages students to learn about the environment and work toward making it cleaner and safer.

The sisters discovered that Bali was one of the world's worst polluters, especially when it came to plastics. And plastic was contributing to the destruction and pollution of oceans around the world. A popular tourist place, Bali is surrounded by the ocean and depends on it for food, transportation and tourism.

They also learned about inspirational people such as South Africa's anti-**apartheid** leader Nelson Mandela and India's Mahatma Gandhi, who led a movement for independence through peaceful protest. This gave them ideas about how they too could make a difference.

They gathered names on a petition, raised awareness and spread information to primary schools in Indonesia. "We went forward with a pure passion and intention to make our island home plastic-bag free," said Melati.

Their first organization led to one called Mountain Mamas, which teaches women in the mountains of Bali how to make bags from donated and recycled materials.

The girls got a lot of attention on social media. They continued to speak up about plastic pollution and pressure the Bali government.

In 2018 the government promised to phase out single-use plastic bags. And in June 2019, they did!

AHA!

Beware of Plastics!

Why is plastic so harmful to the environment? It takes hundreds of years for plastic to break down. In the meantime, it fills our soil and water with harmful chemicals. Wildlife can choke on larger plastics or be poisoned if they consume it, as plastics contain and absorb toxic chemicals. Mountains of plastic have been found in oceans around the world, where they break down into microplastics—bits of plastic so small that they are hard to see with the naked eye.

Melati and Isabel Wijsen lead a movement in Bali to take action against climate change and reduce plastic everywhere.

Juergen Schau

DAVID Shepherd
TRAVIS PRICE

PINK SHIRT DAY.CA
coastcapital

GirlsCo.

Anjali Katta

CHAPTER THREE
NOTICE WHAT'S NEEDED

Eileen Wani Wingfield was an Australian Aboriginal elder born around 1935. When she was in her 20s, she noticed Aboriginal people going blind, developing cancer and dying young. Years later people realized these were symptoms of radiation sickness. Wingfield's people were exposed to the deadly radiation from nuclear tests held in southern Australia in the 1950s and 1960s.

In the 1990s the Australian government wanted to build a radioactive waste dump in South Australia. Wingfield joined the Kupa Piti Kungka Tjuta, a council of senior Aboriginal women from the town of Coober Pedy, and traveled the country, protesting the project.

Thanks to the council's work, the government abandoned plans to build the dump. In 2003 Wingfield won the Goldman Environmental Prize, one of the world's top prizes for environmental activists.

Sometimes the first step in becoming an accidental activist is as simple as recognizing a problem. The second step is doing what you can to solve it.

Mr. Floatie was the mascot for activists raising a stink about the dumping of raw sewage, including human poop, into the waters off Victoria, British Columbia. Mr. Floatie stood more than two meters (six feet) tall, was brown and looked like, well, you know what. He began protesting in 2004, pointing out that the lack of proper sewage treatment was hurting the region's ocean ecosystem, endangering creatures from killer whales to shellfish.

Mr. Floatie retired in 2017 when construction finally began on a sewage treatment plant for the area. Besides, he was pooped...

TAKE ACTION

GONE BUT NOT FORGOTTEN

It was noticing a stuffed Tasmanian tiger, or thylacine, in an exhibit in Brighton, England, in 2010 that turned artist Persephone Pearl into an activist. When she saw this extinct animal, she was moved to tears. Then she decided to take action.

A year later Pearl helped organize the first Remembrance Day for Lost Species. Now it's held every year on November 30, and people around the world are encouraged to take part in such activities as planting trees, lighting candles or finding out about Indigenous languages.

HELPING GIRLS AROUND THE WORLD

Anjali Katta
(1997–)

ROYAL ACTIVIST

Harry, Duke of Sussex, joined the Royal Military Academy Sandhurst in 2005 when he was 20 to train as a military officer. Later he noticed how some wounded service personnel struggled to cope with their disabilities and reintegrate into society. Harry became an activist to make sure that injured soldiers are not forgotten.

Harry knew sports can inspire people, so in 2014 he launched the Invictus Games—*invictus* means "unconquered" in Latin. Sick or wounded service personnel from 13 countries, including Canada and the United States, compete in such sports as archery, swimming and wheelchair basketball.

Even as a very young girl, Canadian Anjali Katta noticed how she could help others. She raised money for the British Columbia Children's Hospital by helping in soup kitchens and selling jewelry she had made. But it was on a trip to India, where her parents were born, that Katta was inspired to start her own activism project.

While visiting Mumbai, Katta met girls who couldn't get an education because they were forced to work. Others couldn't go to school because their parents were afraid the boys would harass them. So in 2013 Katta founded GirlsCo. The group works to empower girls locally and globally and bring attention to issues they face. For example, the GirlsCo. project Bombay Pads delivers sex education and menstrual products to girls and women in Mumbai who can't afford them. The latter means that girls can attend school when they have their periods and continue their education.

On the International Day of the Girl Child in 2014, Katta spoke at the United Nations about how strong and capable girls around the world are. The next year she was selected to advise Canada's Girls Advisory Council on what's important to girls.

At GirlsCo. conferences, young people are encouraged to become activists. "I really believe in the ripple effect," said Katta, "that small changes in a community eventually ripple outward and change the consciousness of entire societies."

"Carry out a random act of kindness, with no expectation of reward, safe in the knowledge that one day someone might do the same for you."

—Diana, Princess of Wales (Harry, Duke of Sussex's mother)

Girls around the world have been helped by Anjali Katta and GirlsCo.

SAVING SEABIRDS

Juergen Schau
(1945–)

HELPING HORSES

When Velma Bronn Johnston was driving to work in Nevada one day in 1950, she noticed a truck overcrowded with wild horses. She followed the truck to a **slaughterhouse**, and that's when she became an animal rights activist.

Johnston was soon nicknamed Wild Horse Annie thanks to her campaign to stop the removal of mustangs and donkeys (burros) from public lands. She asked kids to write to politicians. It took Johnston 20 years and thousands of letters, but in 1971 the Wild Free-Roaming Horses and Burros Act was signed into law. This act made it a crime to kill wild horses on most federal land.

In 2004 Juergen Schau and his wife, Elfie, were visiting Witless Bay, in the province of Newfoundland and Labrador. As they walked around the town, they started to notice dead pufflings (baby puffins) on the road. Schau wondered what had happened.

He discovered that pufflings don't see well at night, so they follow the light of the moon to find their way to shore. But when it's foggy or overcast, they get distracted by headlights, store signs or streetlamps. Those lights lead the pufflings onto roads, where they can be hit by cars. Schau felt sorry for the little birds and decided to help them.

Using a butterfly net, the Schaus picked lost pufflings off the road and released them into the ocean. Schau became known as the Puffin Man, and when local kids and neighbors started helping, the Puffin Patrol was created.

Today kids and adults from all over the world go to Newfoundland and Labrador each summer to help the patrol. Using flashlights and nets, they collect the pufflings and take them to the Canadian Parks and Wilderness Society (CPAWS) headquarters. There the seabirds are measured and tagged, so that if they're picked up again, there will be information about their behavior.

The morning after the pufflings are collected, they're placed in ventilated boxes and taken out to sea. There the little birds are gently tossed into the water, and they make their way to the puffin colony at the Witless Bay Ecological Reserve.

Today the Puffin Patrol saves seabirds called petrels too. The group encourages people to turn off unnecessary lights so the birds won't be misdirected.

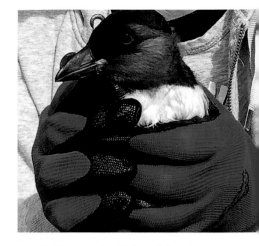

Top: *Pufflings are handled carefully when they're caught and tagged.*

Bottom: *Helping puffins is a great way to be an environmental activist.*

THE SHIRT ON YOUR BACK

Travis Price and David Shepherd
(1990–)

On the first day of high school in 2007, Chuck McNeill of Berwick, Nova Scotia, was bullied for wearing a pink shirt. Twelfth-grade students Travis Price and David Shepherd saw what was happening to the ninth-grade student and decided to take a stand. With some of their friends, they bought all the pink shirts they could find and handed them out at school the next day.

McNeill was amazed when he saw how the other students supported him.

"It looked like a huge weight was lifted off his shoulders," Price said. "I learned that two people can come up with an idea, run with it, and it can do wonders." Schools across Nova Scotia, then throughout Canada and soon around the world took part in the anti-bullying activism that had started accidentally because Price and Shepherd noticed a student in need.

On the last Wednesday in February each year, people in Canada are encouraged to wear a pink shirt to show they're against bullying. Other countries celebrate the International Day of Pink on the second Tuesday in April. Sales of items such as anti-bullying shirts and buttons have also raised money to support programs to end bullying.

Shepherd and Price want to make every day Pink Shirt Day to encourage all people to think about kindness. "We want kids to understand that it's not just about the shirt," said Price. "It's about the everyday actions that they make."

Top: *Travis Price at a Pink Shirt Day event.*

Bottom: *Kids in British Columbia help spread the anti-bullying message on Pink Shirt Day.*

Quinn Callander

Jonah Larson

Pushpa Basnet

CHAPTER FOUR
JUST GET STARTED

Fewer than 300 people speak Koasati, the Indigenous language of the Coushatta Tribe of Louisiana, in the southern United States. Eli Langley cares deeply about keeping his people's language alive. When he was accepted to study at Harvard University, he wanted to use Koasati to fulfill the language requirement of his degree. The university said no.

So Langley started fighting for his language. For more than two years he struggled to change the university's ruling. In 2019, when he was 20, Langley finally succeeded. He believes having Koasati recognized by Harvard is an important step in preserving his language.

There is a saying based on an ancient Chinese proverb: "A journey of a thousand miles begins with a single step." Trying to change the world can seem like a pretty tough task, but sometimes activists just need to begin.

In 1964, Birmingham, Alabama, was one of the most racially divided American cities. Black people were treated unfairly. They had to attend different, inferior schools from white people and weren't allowed in some stores or restaurants. If they complained, their homes could be vandalized.

Black-rights activists held **boycotts**, marches and sit-ins, which resulted in mass arrests. When there weren't enough adults volunteering to be arrested, children participated.

Audrey Faye Hendricks was only nine years old when she took part in the Children's March. She was the youngest person to be arrested, and she was jailed for six days. Hendricks grew up to be an educator, teaching students about the **civil rights movement**, and became known as the Civil Rights Queen.

> **"How wonderful it is that nobody need wait a single moment before starting to improve the world."**
>
> —Anne Frank, author and Holocaust victim

"I'm doing what I can do to give back," says Jonah Larson. "Crochet brings the world together one stitch at a time."

ACCIDENTAL CROCHETER

Jonah Larson
(2008–)

"Hello, crochet friends!" That's how Jonah Larson of La Crosse, Wisconsin, begins his videos. When he was just five years old, his aunt brought him some craft materials, including a crochet hook. Larson was fascinated by it and taught himself to crochet through YouTube videos. He started with a dishcloth, and two years later he was crocheting whole blankets.

Larson started a crochet business called Jonah's Hands. With the money he makes selling his crafts, he helps the orphanage in Ethiopia in which he lived until he was adopted by an American family when he was five months old. Larson creates everything from hats and stuffed animals to sweaters and baskets. He has become a social-media star, and he uses his fame to raise money for other projects in Ethiopia.

"Giving back to the community is very important to me," said Larson. He loves to read, and in 2019 he

TAKE ACTION

CRAFTY ACTIVISM

Do you like crafts and feel too shy to be an activist? Maybe the Craftivist Collective, based in London, England, is for you. Started by cross-stitcher Sarah Corbett in 2009, the gentle protest group creates crafted messages of encouragement, peace and solidarity that they leave in public places.

On the Craftivist Collective website you can find out about making banners, stitching messages onto handkerchiefs, sewing a heart with a message and more. "If we want a world that is beautiful, kind and fair," said Corbett, "shouldn't our activism be beautiful, kind and fair?"

Jonah Larson crochets blankets with many designs. In 2020 he created one with the letters BLM for Black Lives Matter (see page 65) and another, for the COVID-19 pandemic, that read Stay Home.

started a GoFundMe page to raise money for a library in the village where he was born.

Follow Larson on Instagram and watch the videos on his YouTube channel to see how amazingly fast this accidental activist can crochet even extremely complicated patterns. His book *Hello, Crochet Friends!* celebrates Larson's favorite craft, as well as the importance of acceptance, friendship and kindness. "I see crochet as a positive way to bring the world together," said Larson, "and it's just a craft that everybody comes together and enjoys."

Top: *Jonah Larson often talks about creating change for the better.*

Bottom: *Larson has won hundreds of awards for his crochet work and designs.*

HELPING THE HELPERS

Feed the Frontlines
(2020–)
and Quinn Callander
(2008–)

During the COVID-19 **pandemic**, many activists sprang into action to help keep the virus from spreading. They also found ways to assist the doctors, nurses and other frontline staff who were so busy fighting the virus in hospitals and other facilities.

These frontline workers had no time to shop for food or prepare healthy meals for themselves. Organizations such as Feed the Frontlines were started in cities around the world, including London, New York, Toronto and Vancouver, to provide these heroes with delicious, nutritious meals from local restaurants. To thank the frontline workers for their service, people donated money to pay for the meals, and restaurants cooked and delivered the food.

Feed the Frontlines and similar groups helped restaurants that were struggling since people could no longer come in to buy a meal. The food programs enabled the eateries to stay open and keep their employees working.

Many groups helped fight the coronavirus in other ways. For instance, a clothing company switched to making surgical gowns, a perfume maker produced hand sanitizer, and a factory making cell-phone parts began manufacturing surgical masks. These businesses often gave out their products for free. Another way people helped was by shopping for elderly neighbors who couldn't go outside.

Quinn Callander, a teen from Maple Ridge, British Columbia, used his 3D printer to create ear guards that made surgical masks much more comfortable to wear. The guards are attached to the straps of masks to take pressure off the backs of wearers' ears. Callander donated the ear guards to doctors and nurses in his neighborhood and mailed them to workers in the United States, the United Kingdom, Singapore and other places around the world.

> **"I had an idea and I ran with it. People jumped on board and together we fed thousands. Don't overthink things— just go for it."**
> —Adair Roberts, founder, Feed the Frontlines TO

Quinn Callander has motivated thousands of people with 3D printers to create ear guards and help more frontline workers.

PRISON BREAK

Pushpa Basnet
(1984–)

WHAT'S GLOCAL?

All of us—kids and adults—are encouraged to "think globally, act locally." That means an action you take in your community can lead to change and improvement in your city. And that can spread to your larger region, then your country and even the world. This idea has led to the new word "glocal," which combines "global" and "local."

At college in Kathmandu, Nepal, Pushpa Basnet studied social work. She was just 21 when, in 2005, she visited a prison for a school assignment. There she was shocked to see babies and children living behind bars with their imprisoned mothers. These moms had no one to look after their kids—if the children didn't live in prison, they'd have to live on the street all by themselves.

Basnet was determined to change this tragic situation. "No child should grow up behind prison bars," she said. On May 24, 2005, she founded the Early Childhood Development Center (ECDC) and, with her sister and friends, quickly raised money to start a day-care program.

The kids at the prison call her Mamu—it means "mother" in Nepali. These kids have no access to education, good food, medical care or warm clothing, so the ECDC provides them.

Since 2007 kids old enough to be separated from their moms have been able to live at a home outside the prison. It's a safe place for them to live and play, and they still get together with their moms.

The ECDC also assists imprisoned moms by helping them get an education, and since 2009 Basnet has been teaching them to create crafts so the women can make some money. She and the ECDC work hard to provide kids and their moms with a home, a life and a future.

Pushpa Basnet (left) provides children of prisoners with not only a home, but also free food and schooling.

Abisoye
Ajayi-
Akinfolarin

SEVERN
CULLIS
SUZUKI

DOLORES
HUERTA

CHAPTER FIVE
BE AN EXPERT

Andrei Sakharov was a brilliant Russian scientist. While working on **thermonuclear** weapons, he realized these powerful devices could destroy whole cities, killing millions of people, and the radiation they emitted could make our planet unlivable.

Sakharov tried speaking to his superiors about his concerns, but his words were ignored. So Sakharov decided to go public with his views.

The Soviet government was furious. Sakharov lost his job and was banned from leaving the country. His wife, Yelena Bonner, had to accept her husband's 1975 Nobel Peace Prize for him. Yet, despite all the government efforts to silence Sakharov, he continued to speak up.

In 1985 Sakharov went on a hunger strike to help his wife get proper medical treatment. This forced Soviet leader Mikhail Gorbachev to allow Sakharov and his wife to leave Russia for heart surgery. While they were abroad, Gorbachev began to ease his **hard-line** policies. A few months later, when Sakharov and his wife were permitted to return to Russia, Sakharov became an elected member of the government. He continued to push for change.

> "My advice to other disabled people would be, concentrate on things your disability doesn't prevent you from doing well, and don't regret the things it interferes with. Don't be disabled in spirit, as well as physically."
>
> —Stephen Hawking, scientist

Sakharov's knowledge was crucial in convincing people of the dangers of nuclear weapons and the importance of human rights. Knowledge is key to refuting outdated ideas and explaining how change can be a powerful force for everyone's benefit.

Ethiopian lawyer Yetnebersh Nigussie also understands that change through knowledge is essential. Nigussie, blind since age five, advocates for the rights of the disabled and the rights of girls and young women. She wants people to know how capable those with fewer advantages or with disabilities can be if given the chance. "Focus on the person, not the disability," she said. "We have one disability, but 99 abilities to build on." She has brought those ideas to her own country, where about 15 million people live with disabilities.

YOU CAN MAKE IT!

Abisoye Ajayi-Akinfolarin
(1985–)

TAKE ACTION

SOUNDING THE ALARM

In late 2019 ophthalmologist Dr. Li Wenliang sounded the alarm about a new and dangerous coronavirus spreading quickly in Wuhan, China, where he worked. The Wuhan police accused him of making false comments. Dr. Li died of the virus in February 2020. By that time he was being hailed for his heroic stand, even by the Chinese government.

Abisoye Ajayi-Akinfolarin had a difficult childhood. Her mom died when she was four, and her dad beat her often. She knew she had to take care of herself.

When she was 10, she discovered computers, and that changed everything. She loved technology and believed her passion and interest would surely lead her to a well-paid job.

She was right!

After high school Ajayi-Akinfolarin joined a computer company in Nigeria, and she realized she'd found a way out of her difficult circumstances. Her path was set.

As Ajayi-Akinfolarin grew more successful at work, she recognized that working with computers could help other girls find a way out of poverty and harsh family situations. This led her to start an organization, Pearls Africa Youth Foundation, to help young girls develop technology skills through such programs as GirlsCoding.

To find girls interested in changing their lives through education and new skills, Ajayi-Akinfolarin went to some of the toughest and most economically depressed areas of Nigeria—slums, orphanages and even a camp for girls who'd been kidnapped by Boko Haram, a terrorist organization.

She believes that no matter where girls come from or what they've experienced, they can be successful. "They are coders. They are thinkers. Their future is bright," she said.

GirlsCoding has already had success. One girl created an app to help her family's fishing business. The site allowed fishermen to sell directly to buyers. In another project, girls could tell stories about the terror they had experienced with Boko Haram. In 2018 Ajayi-Akinfolarin was the first African to be recognized as a CNN hero, and that recognition has helped her spread the word about her ideas for helping more girls.

AHA!

An Extreme Group

Boko Haram is an extreme and **militant** Islamic group based in Nigeria whose purpose is to promote **Sharia law**. Members of Boko Haram have killed thousands of people in pursuit of their goal.

"Learning to write programs stretches your mind and helps you think better."
—Bill Gates, cofounder of Microsoft

These girls in Nigeria are coding their way to success.

Dolores Huerta is proud of her Mexican American heritage.

SI, SE PUEDE— YES, WE CAN

Dolores Huerta

(1930–)

Dolores Huerta was a good student, a Girl Scout, an accomplished writer, dancer, pianist and violinist. Despite all these achievements, as a Mexican American she faced **racism** and **discrimination**. One of her teachers didn't think a Mexican girl could be very smart and accused her of cheating because her paper was so well written.

But Huerta kept studying and working. She went to college and became a teacher. While teaching poor kids in farming communities, she realized how much discrimination and poverty affected the Latino community. "They didn't have toilets in the field," she said. "They didn't have cold drinking water. They didn't have rest periods."

She had to do something more to help. She resigned her teaching job and became an activist for change.

For the next 50 years, Huerta used her knowledge of the difficult conditions farmworkers faced to help improve their lives. She cofounded with César Chávez

NEVER GIVE UP

CÉSAR CHÁVEZ

César Chávez was an American who dedicated his life to improving the treatment, pay and working conditions of farmworkers. He worked for years alongside Dolores Huerta.

"Dolores was very gracious when I told her I had 'stolen' her slogan, 'Si, se puede. Yes, we can.'"

—Barack Obama
44th president of the United States

> "We cannot seek achievement for ourselves and forget about progress and prosperity for our community."
> —César Chávez, labor organizer

> "Every moment is an organizing opportunity, every person a potential activist, every minute a chance to change the world."
> —Dolores Huerta

Dolores Huerta marches for human rights. She never gives up.

what would eventually become the United Farm Workers of America. She worked tirelessly to make working conditions better for grape workers and lettuce pickers. She advocated for workers so they wouldn't be exposed to hazardous pesticides that endangered their health and the health of their families. She encouraged everyone to vote so all their voices would be heard.

Huerta kept coming up with ideas and strategies, organizing rallies and protests even though the struggle for fairness was often dangerous. In 1988 she was severely beaten by San Francisco police during a peaceful rally. That landed her in the hospital, but it didn't stop her work.

Huerta coined the phrase "si, se puede," which is Spanish for "yes, we can," as a rallying cry during protests. Those powerful words inspired Barack Obama in his campaign to become president of the United States. He acknowledged Huerta's leadership and skill in 2012 when he awarded her the Presidential Medal of Freedom, the highest civilian award in the United States.

Barack Obama recognizes Dolores Huerta for her contributions by awarding her the Presidential Medal of Freedom. In his speech he thanked her for letting him use her phrase "Si, se puede" ("Yes, we can") to inspire people around the world.

Severn Cullis-Suzuki lives on beautiful Haida Gwaii, on the northern Pacific coast of Canada.

FIGHTING FOR MY FUTURE

Severn Cullis-Suzuki

(1979–)

Ever since she was a little girl, Severn Cullis-Suzuki has been passionate about the environment. The daughter of well-known environmentalists David Suzuki and Tara Cullis, Cullis-Suzuki wanted other kids to learn about the importance of fighting climate change, protecting endangered animals, keeping our air clean and our water safe to drink. At age nine she started the Environmental Children's Organization to do just that.

When she was 12, Cullis-Suzuki and her friends raised enough money through her organization to fly to the 1992 Earth Summit conference in Rio de Janeiro, where she gave a speech that earned her the title "the girl who silenced the world for five minutes." Her words were passionate and clear. "I am fighting for my future," she said. She talked about going fishing in Vancouver with her dad and finding fish full of cancers, and about animals and plants vanishing every day. "I have dreamt of seeing the great herds of wild animals, jungles and rainforests

Severn Cullis-Suzuki's amazing parents, environmentalists Tara Cullis and David Suzuki.

full of birds and butterflies," she said, "but now I wonder if they will even exist for my children to see."

Cullis-Suzuki told the scientists and politicians, "If you don't know how to fix it, please stop breaking it."

After graduating from Yale University with a bachelor of science in ecology and evolutionary biology, Cullis-Suzuki helped launch an internet-based **think tank** called the Skyfish Project to share ideas about preserving the environment. She continued to write and speak about the importance of the natural world.

She lives with her husband and children on Haida Gwaii, home of the Haida Nation. Many Indigenous languages are only fluently spoken by a few people and are in danger of being lost, so Cullis-Suzuki is learning Haida from the Elders. She is now teaching it to others, hoping to help the Haida people preserve their language and culture for the future.

AHA!

Beautiful Islands

Haida Gwaii is an archipelago of 150 islands off the northwest coast of British Columbia. It's hard to reach and hauntingly beautiful. It's full of diverse animal and plant life and hardy people. The totem poles in the Indigenous villages here are some of the oldest in the world.

These historic totem poles still stand on Haida Gwaii.

BLACK LIVES MATTER

OPAL TOMETI

ALICIA GARZA

PATRISSE KHAN-CULLORS

TEGAN and SARA QUIN

Autumn Peltier

CHAPTER SIX
STAY FOCUSED

Izidor Ruckel was just one of thousands of orphans neglected and mistreated in orphanages in Romania. He was adopted by an American couple in 1991, when he was 11 years old. His parents soon discovered that Ruckel needed several surgeries to help him overcome the effects of **polio**, a paralyzing disease. Despite his health issues, Ruckel wanted to help other orphans. In his early 20s he began advocating for kids without parents and made people aware of the difficult lives some of them have.

Successful activists know that it's not enough to get started—you've got to keep going and concentrate on making changes, no matter what obstacles you face.

In 1997, when Elizabeth Bloomer was 12 years old, she learned about Iqbal Masih, a Pakistani boy sold into slavery by his parents when he was only four years old. Bloomer was so upset at how some children are abused that she vowed to do something about it. She worked with the kids at her school in Quincy, Massachusetts, to raise money to build a school in Masih's village. "You are never too young to take action," she said.

With her talent for public speaking, Bloomer has given talks about child labor, including at the United Nations in 2001. At university she stayed focused on helping kids, speaking out and encouraging others to help stop the abuse of children. "I've realized the power kids have to make a difference," she said.

AHA!

Peace Love Bracelets

Bella Fricker of Alpharetta, Georgia, was nine years old in 2016 when she noticed that one of the American Girl dolls didn't have hair. This doll was made especially for kids who'd lost their hair during cancer treatment. Fricker wanted to buy some of those dolls to give to young patients. But how could she raise money to buy them?

Fricker made bracelets that her mom sold on Facebook. Soon she was giving away dolls and starting the Peace Love Bracelets Foundation Inc. Fricker was diagnosed with Type 1 juvenile **diabetes** in 2017 but has stayed focused on activism, even giving away diabetes care kits.

> **"Never doubt that a small group of thoughtful, committed citizens can change the world; indeed, it's the only thing that ever has."**
>
> —Margaret Mead, anthropologist

Tegan (left) and Sara began playing guitar and writing songs when they were just 15 years old.

TWIN POWER

Tegan and Sara Quin

(1980–)

You've probably sung along with Tegan and Sara's hit song "Everything Is Awesome!!!" from *The LEGO Movie*. These twin sisters from Calgary, Alberta, are famous around the world and have won many awards. They've headlined shows everywhere and have performed at major festivals such as Coachella, Lollapalooza and Glastonbury. Both are singers and songwriters who play many instruments.

But activism is important to Tegan and Sara too. The sisters both identify as queer and have used their fame to advocate for **LGBTQ+** equality. They have also donated money and fundraised for gay rights. They founded the Tegan and Sara Foundation in 2016 to support issues especially important to LGBTQ+ girls and women, such as speaking out about discrimination, getting help with mental-health issues and advocating for marriage equality. In 2018 they met with Canadian prime minister Justin Trudeau and members

TAKE ACTION

CIRCLE OF LOVE

When world-famous singer and songwriter Annie Lennox was visiting South Africa in 2003, she became aware of how many women and children were affected by the human immunodeficiency virus (**HIV**) and acquired immune deficiency syndrome (**AIDS**). The Scottish performer was inspired to become an activist and help give these people a voice.

Lennox's charity, the Circle, raises money and awareness to help women and girls around the world. The organization fights injustice, helps promote education, works to improve health and more.

of the country's Parliament to discuss how the government can be a world leader in supporting equal rights for LGBTQ+ people.

Tegan and Sara are committed to their activism but don't feel they're doing anything that other people can't do. "I don't feel brave because I sing about dating a girl," said Sara. "For me, bravery is being a doctor or a teacher or a politician."

Onstage, Tegan and Sara talk about their activism, their childhood and what it's like to tour.

At first the twins called their band Sara and Tegan. But people thought they were a solo act called Sara Antegan. The sisters switched the names around, and the band started to take off.

WATER WARRIOR

Autumn Peltier

(2004–)

NEVER GIVE UP

A FAMILY OF ACTIVISTS

Autumn Peltier's great-aunt Josephine Mandamin inspired her to become an activist. In 2003 Mandamin heard a prophecy from an Elder that water would be as valuable as gold by the year 2030. Like other Anishinaabe people, Mandamin believed that grandmothers had the responsibility of leading other women to protect water.

She started the water walk movement to bring attention to the importance of clean water. Before she died in 2019, she had walked the shorelines of all the Great Lakes—a distance of about 17,000 miles (27,360 kilometers).

More than 100 Indigenous communities across Canada don't have water that is safe to drink. Anishinaabe activist Autumn Peltier fights for clean water. A member of the Wiikwemkoong First Nation on Manitoulin Island in northern Ontario, Peltier travels around the world speaking out about the need for clean drinking water.

In the fall of 2015, Peltier and youth advocate Francesca Pheasant, also from Wiikwemkoong, represented Canada at the Children's Climate Conference in Sweden. There they talked about how global warming is hurting the planet and causing water shortages.

The next year Peltier brought her message to a meeting of Canada's premiers. She helped her great-aunt Josephine Mandamin (see sidebar) perform a water ceremony, sang a water song and spoke to Prime Minister Justin Trudeau about her climate concerns.

In March 2018 Peltier spoke at the United Nations on World Water Day. "One day I will be an ancestor,"

"Our people are caretakers of the land and waters," Autumn Peltier says. "Everything is connected and depending on clean water."

she said, "and I want to leave a legacy for my great-grandchildren so they know I worked hard to ensure they have a future." She was back at the UN in September 2019, speaking at the United Nations Global Landscapes Forum. Peltier emphasized to her audience that water is vital, reminding them that people can't eat money or drink oil.

Peltier is known as a "water warrior." "We are water," she said. "We come from water—and when the water is sick, we are sick."

"Nothing can live without water," says Autumn Peltier. "If we don't act now there will come a time when we will be fighting for those last barrels of water."

Left: *"We come from a place where we are surrounded by the freshest water in the world," says Autumn Peltier, "and it's at risk of being contaminated."*

BLACK LIVES MATTER

Alicia Garza,
(1981–)

Patrisse Khan-Cullors
(1984–)

and Opal Tometi
(1984–)

When George Zimmerman, who identifies as Hispanic, was **acquitted** in the 2012 shooting death of Black teenager Trayvon Martin in Florida, Black people across the United States protested. Alicia Garza, a youth and human rights activist in the San Francisco area, wrote a Facebook post she called "A Love Note to Black People." It included the phrase "Our Lives Matter, Black Lives Matter." That inspired Patrisse Khan-Cullors, an artist and prison rights activist, to reply, "#Black Lives Matter." When Opal Tometi, a writer and community organizer, added

Left: Demonstrators at a Black Lives Matter protest on June 1, 2020, in London, England.

her support, the Black Lives Matter movement was born.

The group supports people speaking out against the inequalities and violence that Black people face. It encourages people to build a world where Black lives really do matter.

Black Lives Matter holds protests to speak out against police killings of Black people. Perhaps most famously the group organized rallies after George Floyd died in 2020 in Minneapolis, Minnesota, when a white police officer knelt on his neck for almost nine minutes. Protests were held in more than 750 cities around the world.

Some people have criticized Black Lives Matter for dividing people and increasing tension between races. "When we say 'Black Lives Matter,' we're not saying that any other life doesn't matter," said Tometi. "That has never ever been our message. Our message has always been from a place of love."

This rally against racism took place in Berlin, Germany, after the death of George Floyd in the United States on May 25, 2020.

On July 17, 2014, Eric Garner, a Black man, died when a white New York City police officer held him in a chokehold. On the fifth anniversary of his death, people took part in a protest to remember Garner and demand justice.

CHAPTER SEVEN
NETWORKING WORKS

If you want to make positive changes, you need to network and find other people who not only share the same beliefs but are also ready to act, sometimes even despite fierce opposition.

Jacqueline Kennedy Onassis knew that. Educated in France, she admired how that country proudly preserved its beautiful historic buildings. At a time when many old buildings in the United States were being replaced by boxy "modern" structures, she fought to preserve them.

She started her restoration efforts as First Lady of the United States. On February 14, 1962, she led a tour of the White House that was broadcast on TV. To her delight, it was a hit. That warm reception sparked her to advocate for preserving historic Lafayette Square in Washington, DC. She networked with influential people and helped establish the 1966 National Historic Preservation Act.

In 1975 she moved to New York City, where she successfully led the efforts to preserve Grand Central Station, one of the great symbols of New York City.

In Pakistan, Gulalai Ismail also acted to create change. At age 16 she cofounded the organization Aware Girls with her sister, Saba, to stop oppression and violence against rural women.

Girls in Pakistan were being forced into marriages and prevented from getting educations. "Women had few rights and were not permitted to make their own decisions about their lives and futures," Ismail said.

Despite opposition from the government, Ismail trained young women to speak up. Although she won support, awards and admiration from around the world, she was forced to go into hiding. With the help of friends and supporters, she eventually reached the United States in September 2019. She continued to protect women in conflict through Voices for Peace and Democracy, the organization she established after fleeing Pakistan.

MAKE YOUR CITY GREEN

Liz Christy
(1945–1985)

TAKE ACTION

URBAN GARDENS

Urban gardens are sprouting all over Brussels, Belgium. The authors of a guide to Brussels' urban gardens, Christophe and Jacques Mercier, said Liz Christy is their hero and that her example has inspired people all over the world to create urban gardens.

What does someone need to change a community? An energetic, lively personality? Family connections? A kind heart?

Liz Christy had all these things, and they contributed to her becoming an accidental activist.

Christy was an artist who also worked in public relations in New York City. She was a descendant of Frederick Law Olmsted, the designer of Central Park and the father of landscape architecture.

One day in 1973 she saw a seven-year-old boy crawl into an overturned refrigerator in an abandoned lot at the corner of Bowery and Houston Streets. It was a tough, dangerous time in New York City. Across the city, lots like this one were piled with debris and junk.

Christy yanked the boy out of the refrigerator and promised his mom that she would do something to change conditions in the neighborhood. She was determined to make it more livable for everyone.

This neighborhood was in an especially dangerous part of New York, so it was a challenging promise.

But Christy was as good as her word. She'd already formed a group called the Green Guerillas that dropped wildflower seeds into abandoned lots to beautify them. Now she and her friends found soil, manure and plants and began to clear the lot to create a garden. Their work paid off. Their urban garden grew and grew, and that first city garden led to others. Soon Christy's idea had spread all over the city.

By the time she died of cancer at 40, Christy had started an urban garden movement that continues to this day. So does her original garden at Bowery and Houston, which is now a national historic site.

Top: *Step inside and enjoy nature at the Liz Christy Community Garden in New York City. It's a place of beauty, calm and fun in the middle of the bustling city.*

Bottom: *"Liz Christy checks out the urban garden she and her friends created out of an abandoned lot in New York City.*

Joshua Wong faces the Hong Kong police.

GO, HONG KONG

Joshua Wong
(1996–)

The first time Hong Kong student Joshua Wong stood up to the Chinese government, he was only 14 years old. That year Wong cofounded a movement to protest the school curriculum China had imposed on Hong Kong. Wong and his friends drew thousands of students to their cause, and these huge protests caused China to back down.

In 2014 Wong was an important leader in another protest called the umbrella movement, in which umbrellas were used both as protection from pepper spray and as a symbol of resistance. Hong Kong protesters wanted China to stop imposing its politics on their city—they wanted their voices to be heard through a democratic election. The movement drew a large number of supporters. "One person, one vote, is just the starting point for democracy," said Wong. China did not back down this time, and Wong was arrested.

He was determined to keep fighting for a democratic Hong Kong, although he realized it was an uphill battle

NEVER GIVE UP

JOIN HANDS

The Hong Kong Way demonstration on August 23, 2019, saw thousands of protesters join hands in a 30-mile (50-kilometer) human chain around the city to protest China's oppression. The event was inspired by the Baltic Way in 1989, when two million people in Latvia, Lithuania and Estonia formed a human chain to mark 50 years of freedom from the Soviet Union. The Baltic Way has inspired freedom fighters around the world. "It demonstrates the power of solidarity and nonviolent social movements," said Joshua Wong.

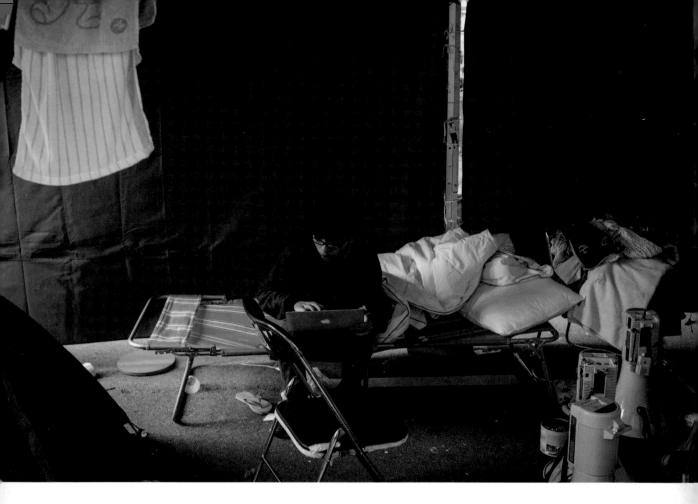

Joshua Wong proves that you can lead a protest from almost anywhere.

against a powerful, well-armed China. Nevertheless, Wong and other young people in Hong Kong felt they had no choice. It was their future, and they wanted to stand up and be heard.

The protests continued and grew. They mostly were peaceful, but sometimes there were violent clashes between Chinese police and protesters. On November 24, 2019, 2.9 million people turned out to vote in Hong Kong, giving a **landslide** victory to the pro-democracy parties. The struggle for democracy in Hong Kong continues even though many protestors have been arrested and oppressive new laws have been imposed by the current Chinese government.

Joshua Wong and many others bravely march for the future of Hong Kong and their democratic rights.

THEN THEY CAME FOR ME

Maziar Bahari

(1967–)

Growing up in Iran, Maziar Bahari knew the importance and dangers of standing up to tyranny. His father had been imprisoned by the Shah of Iran's regime in the 1950s, and his sister had been arrested by the revolutionary government of Ayatollah Khomeini in the 1980s.

In 1988 Bahari immigrated to Canada to study communications. Soon after graduating from university, he made *The Voyage of the St. Louis*, a film about a ship carrying 937 Jews escaping from the brutal **Nazi** regime in 1939. The ship was turned back by Cuba, the United States and Canada, and most of the people who were forced to return to Germany died in the Holocaust.

Why did a young man from Iran feel drawn to this story? Bahari says it was his teacher at Concordia University in Montreal who taught him about the discrimination Jews have faced through the ages. And having grown up in a Jewish neighborhood in Iran, Bahari identified with people who were treated unfairly by their government. He went on to make other award-winning documentaries.

In 1998 he became *Newsweek* magazine's Iran correspondent. In 2009, while working in Iran, he was arrested and imprisoned as a spy. He was not a spy, but he was forced to confess. He was finally released with help from the US government, after publicity for his cause had appeared in newspapers around the world.

Following his release, Bahari spoke and wrote about his ordeal. He also began a campaign to help other jailed journalists and to advance human rights. He launched IranWire, a citizen journalism news site, to empower other Iranians. He published a memoir of his experiences called *Then They Came for Me*. The title comes from the writings of Pastor Martin Niemöller and conveys how important it is to speak out against abuse, discrimination and tyranny. Niemöller's poem "First they came…" ends with the line "Then they came for me—and there was no one left to speak for me."

AHA!

Unfair!

Many journalists are unfairly imprisoned around the world because of their honest reporting. Between July 2016 and November 2019, Turkey jailed more journalists than any other country in the world.

Maziar Bahari speaks up for journalists around the world who've been unfairly imprisoned, silenced or worse.

PETE SEEGER
Kailash Satyarthi
WE DEMAND EQUAL RIGHTS NOW!
FREEDOM
KATIE EDER
ENOUGH

CHAPTER EIGHT
BE FLEXIBLE

Staying true to your values while being flexible is difficult but key to making the world a better place.

Journalist, social activist and human rights advocate June Callwood recognized that from the time she was a young girl. Callwood grew up in Canada during the Depression, a time of radical economic and social change. Her parents had trouble supporting the family, so she had learned how to fend for herself by the time she was in her teens.

Callwood became a journalist, freelance writer, wife and mother. When her son Barney was living in a **hippie** section of Toronto, she met some of his friends who were runaways and addicted to drugs. She wanted to help, and this was the start of her work as a social activist. Callwood eventually helped establish more than 50 organizations to help a range of people in need—the poor, the disadvantaged, struggling artists and writers, the elderly and people with life-threatening illnesses.

> **"The art of life is a constant readjustment to our surroundings."**
>
> —Kakuzo Okakaura, Japanese scholar

Successful activists like Callwood know that everything changes. They know they might have to alter their plans to reflect new situations.

This was true of Shirin Ebadi, an Iranian political and human rights activist and a former judge who has worked tirelessly to promote rights for all. Conservative clerics in Iran forced her out of her position as a judge because she was a woman. Ebadi kept fighting to regain that position while working as a lawyer, writing about the law and her beliefs, and representing people who stood up to the repressive Iranian government.

For her human rights work, she was awarded the 2003 Nobel Peace Prize, but instead of celebrating their citizen, the Iranian government attacked, imprisoned and shunned Ebadi. She left Iran for her own safety but has continued to speak out.

EVERYONE DESERVES A CHANCE

Kailash Satyarthi

(1954–)

> **"Knowing what must be done does away with fear."**
> —Rosa Parks,
> civil rights activist

> **"It takes a village to raise a child."**
> —African proverb

Kailash Satyarthi grew up in a middle-class family in a small town in India. Although his mother wasn't educated, she believed that everyone deserved a chance in life. Her attitude influenced her young son. He understood that children from privileged homes like his had better access to schools and opportunities for education. He knew that many poor children couldn't go to school because they had to work to help their families survive.

Although there were many poor people in his village, both Muslims and Hindus, people lived peacefully together. That positive atmosphere influenced Satyarthi.

After he had completed studies in engineering, he began to teach. He soon realized that it wasn't what he really wanted to do. In 1980 he gave up his career and founded the Bachpan Bachao Andolan (Movement to Save Childhood). Since then he's led global marches against child labor and child slavery. He has set up many organizations that strive to give poor children access to education and a decent life. "Every single minute matters, every single child matters, every single childhood matters," he said.

In 1986 his tireless marching and speaking efforts led to changes in India's child labor laws. In 2014 Satyarthi was awarded the Nobel Peace Prize for his work.

"History will judge us by the difference we make in the everyday lives of children."

—Nelson Mandela, freedom fighter and former president of South America

Malala Yousafzai and Kailash Satyarthi accept their Nobel Peace Prizes.

MUSIC LIFTS US UP

Pete Seeger

(1919–2014)

As a child Peter Seeger heard music everywhere. His family members were musicians, and he often traveled with them around the United States. When he was 16, he fell in love with the banjo while at a festival in Asheville, North Carolina.

Although Seeger decided to study journalism at Harvard, his love of music and his belief in social activism led him to change direction. He was inspired by the music and activism of singer-songwriters like Woody Guthrie, and he was one of the original members of the Weavers, a traditional folk quartet. "A good song reminds us what we're fighting for," he said. Seeger was determined to entertain people and share his belief that everyone should be treated with dignity and fairness. "If there's something wrong, speak up," he said.

It wasn't easy. After World War II there was an anti-communist wave in the United States. Many artists' and writers' reputations were damaged, and many careers were destroyed. Seeger's career also suffered when he

AHA!

We Shall Overcome

Many people think the famous protest song "We Shall Overcome" was influenced by a gospel hymn first published in 1900 by African American minister Charles Albert Tindley. The song was linked to the civil rights movement in 1959, when Guy Carawan and Pete Seeger's version was performed.

Left: Pete Seeger never stopped singing or standing up for what he believed in—human rights and peace.

Pete Seeger shares talk, music and stories.

refused to speak against his fellow artists. He almost went to jail.

In 1962 the American government finally dropped its charges against Seeger, and he increased his social activism. He marched for civil rights and against apartheid. He reworked the song "We Shall Overcome," which became a ballad for freedom movements. He spoke up against the Vietnam War. In the 1960s he took his boat, *Clearwater*, and worked tirelessly to clean up his beloved Hudson River. His efforts made a huge difference and inspired many others.

Pete Seeger touched hearts around the world with his music and words of peace.

ACTION NOW

Katie Eder

(1999–)

When Katie Eder was injured and could no longer compete as a figure skater, her parents encouraged her to take a writing course.

Write? She'd never liked writing book reports or doing assignments in school. But to her surprise, she found creative writing was different. She loved writing in her own voice and expressing her ideas. At 13 that passion led Eder to start Kids Tales, an organization that holds writing workshops for youth in underserved communities. It began with 10 kids in a community center in Milwaukee, Wisconsin, and has spread globally. Kids Tales stories are published in an anthology and sold on Amazon.

Eder's activism didn't end there. After the horrific shooting in 2018 at Marjory Stoneman Douglas High School in Parkland, Florida, she was inspired by the Parkland students' activism and their March for Our Lives. So Eder created 50 Miles More. Her group walked

50 miles (80.5 kilometers) in Wisconsin to demand that politicians act on gun violence.

And if those two organizations weren't enough, Eder became director of Future Coalition, a large network of youth-led organizations and leaders that works to create change in their communities and around the world, speaking up about such issues as climate change. Eder became aware of the need for action on climate after reading Al Gore's book *An Inconvenient Truth*.

Eder sees all these organizations focused on change as connected and important. "This is the revolution that's going to save our planet," she said. "Our generation is not going to sit around as our futures are destroyed around us."

Katie Eder calls for action! Now!

Will Connolly

Lilly Singh

CLARA HUGHES

CHAPTER NINE
BE UNSTOPPABLE

Poaching is a real problem in Africa. Poachers kill as many as 100 elephants every day for the animals' ivory and meat. The Black Mambas Anti-Poaching Unit is a mostly female team of park rangers. Set up in 2013, the group is named after a deadly African snake. But these Black Mambas work hard to stop poaching of elephants, lions, rhinoceroses and other animals on South Africa's **savannas**. The members learned how to survive there, how to spot animal traps and what to do when they meet a lion. They are also trained in combat, first aid and communication.

At first the group faced a lot of opposition. "They were all saying, 'What are they thinking? Women cannot do this—this is a man's job,'" said Felicia Mogakane, one of the Black Mambas. "But we have proved them wrong."

Many accidental activists have faced obstacles as they try to make the world a better place. But they learn to overcome difficulties to accomplish their goals.

Henry Bergh was a wealthy American diplomat who had never even owned a pet. But in 1863, when he saw a horse being beaten in the streets of St. Petersburg, Russia, he became a crusader for the rights of animals. "I made up my mind," Bergh said, "that when I came home I would **prosecute** those who **persecuted** poor dumb beasts."

> **"Mercy to animals means mercy to mankind."**
> —Henry Bergh, founder of the ASPCA

Three years later he founded the American Society for the Prevention of Cruelty to Animals (ASPCA), the first humane society in North America. In 1875, after discovering that many children also were being abused, Bergh started the New York Society for the Prevention of Cruelty to Children. It was the world's first child-protection agency.

EGG-CELLENT ACTIVIST

Will "Egg Boy" Connolly

(2002–)

On March 15, 2019, a gunman attacked mosques in Christchurch, New Zealand, killing 51 people and injuring 49 others. The next day Australian senator Fraser Anning spoke at a news conference in Melbourne, Australia, and blamed the attacks on the immigration of "Muslim fanatics."

This racist remark infuriated many people at the event, including Will "Egg Boy" Connolly. The 17-year-old was so disgusted by Anning's divisive language that he couldn't stop himself. He walked up behind Anning and cracked an egg over his head. "I understand what I did was not the right thing to do," Connolly said afterward. "However, this egg has united people."

People figured Anning would take Connolly to court, so Egg Boy supporters around the world quickly began fundraising to pay for Connolly's legal costs—and buy more eggs! A law firm offered to help Connolly for free, but in the end he didn't face any charges. (Anning punched Connolly after the egging, and the senator's supporters tackled Connolly to the ground, but Anning wasn't charged either.)

So Connolly donated all the money that had been raised—more than $93,000—to help the people who'd been injured in the shooting and their families. He hoped the donation would make them feel supported and give them assistance with their medical bills and other needs. Connolly encourages everyone to fight hate speech.

"You can't always measure the effects of activist work; you just have to wish and pray that the message gets through."

—Yoko Ono, artist

Will Connolly (middle) was shocked when he became famous. "Too much of the attention is brought away from the real victims suffering— we should be focusing on them," he said.

SUPERWOMAN

Lilly Singh

(1988–)

YouTube star, actor and comedian Lilly Singh may seem confident, but she didn't always feel that way. Singh grew up in Scarborough, Ontario, in a Punjabi family. She studied **psychology** at university, but after she graduated she didn't know what she wanted to do. Singh was suffering from **depression**, and in 2010 she started making YouTube videos to help her cope with these negative feelings.

Singh chose the nickname Superwoman because she'd imagined as a kid that she had a big invisible S for *super* on her chest. That belief had made her feel she could do anything.

Sharing the feeling that girls and women can accomplish anything became important to Singh, so in 2016 she started her campaign #GirlLove. This movement encourages girls and women to think positively and support each other. Singh was able to get other celebrities to help spread her message and talk about how cool it is for women to help one another.

Singh knows how important education is for girls in developing countries, so she helps raise money for this

NEVER GIVE UP

RYAN'S WELLS

In 1998, Ryan Hreljac learned what a difficult time many Africans have getting clean water. So the six-year-old from Kemptville, Ontario, began raising money to help. In just a year Hreljac collected $2,000, enough to drill a well in Uganda.

Four years later Hreljac set up the Ryan's Well Foundation to help people in many developing countries. The organization builds wells and sanitary latrines in Africa, Central America and South Asia, and educates kids about clean water. Hreljac's group has helped more than one million people. For his activism, he was the youngest person to earn the Order of Ontario, the province's top honor.

cause. She promotes the purchase of #GirlLove Rafiki bracelets, which are handmade by girls in Kenya. Money from bracelet sales gives girls the opportunity to go to school, as well as encouraging them to help each other.

Singh continues to speak out and break down barriers. In September 2019 she became the first woman of color and the first openly bisexual person to host a late-night talk show on a major American television network.

Lilly Singh has been a UNICEF Goodwill Ambassador, advocating for the rights of children.

NONSTOP OLYMPIAN

Clara Hughes

(1972–)

Not only is Clara Hughes one of the only athletes in the world to have competed in both the Winter and Summer Olympic Games, but she's also the only person ever to have won more than one medal in both games. At the Winter Games she competed for Canada in speed skating, and in the Summer Games she won medals in road cycling. Only one other Canadian athlete (Cindy Klassen) has won as many Olympic medals as Hughes has.

You might think someone who's accomplished so much would feel unstoppable. But for years Hughes hid the fact that she suffered from severe depression. Eventually she decided to use her fame to become an advocate for others who suffer from the same illness.

In 2010 Hughes became the national spokesman for Bell Canada's Let's Talk program. She wanted to end the stigma that caused people with mental illness to feel ashamed. Hughes set off on her "Big Ride" in 2014,

Left: *Clara Hughes (middle), Kristina Groves (left) and Cindy Klassen compete at the 2006 Winter Olympics in Turin, Italy. They earned a silver medal in the speed-skating team pursuit.*

NEVER GIVE UP

RUNNING FOR PEACE

When Tegla Loroupe was growing up in Kenya, her father wouldn't allow her to attend school. She went anyway, even though it meant running 6 miles (10 kilometers) to and from school daily. Loroupe became such a good runner that in 1994 she was the first African woman to win the New York Marathon.

Loroupe used her fame to become a champion for peace in northern Kenya and other African countries. She started the Tegla Loroupe Peace Foundation in 2003. It uses sport to promote good will and gender equality.

biking more than 6,835 miles (11,000 kilometers) across Canada to raise awareness about mental health.

Hughes was also an honorary witness of the Truth and Reconciliation Commission, which operated from 2008 to 2015. It documented the history and impact of residential schools on students and families. These schools were set up by the Canadian government and run by churches. For more than 100 years, Indigenous kids were taken from their families and culture and put into schools where they were abused emotionally and often physically. Clara was proud to take part in the Commission and help work for justice for residential school survivors.

Clara Hughes competes in road cycling at the 2012 Olympic Games in London, England.

At the 2010 Olympic Games in Vancouver, BC, Hughes was a flag bearer. She led the Canadian team into the opening ceremony.

WILLIAM

KAMKWAMBA

Rigoberta
Menchú Tum

ប្រយ័ត្នត្រាប់មីន!!

Danger!! Mines!!

Song
Kosal

CHAPTER TEN
DREAM BIG

Farlis Calle Guerrero was just 15 years old in 1996 when her friend was killed during the **civil war** that had raged for decades in her home country of Colombia. With the help of the United Nations Children's Fund (UNICEF), Guerrero and other young people organized a children's peace movement and held a special countrywide election in which Colombian youth cast votes for 12 basic rights, including the right to peace. Experts had estimated that about 500,000 kids would turn out. But on October 25, 1996, 2.7 million kids voted, despite death threats and intimidation. "You can't kill the hopes of kids," said Guerrero.

> **"We can't change the whole world alone, but if I can teach people that if you put your hand in mine and little by little we join more hands, maybe we can construct a new world."**
>
> —Farlis Calle Guerrero, activist

Sometimes making the world a better place can seem like an overwhelming job. That's when it's important to set ambitious goals. Even if you don't quite make all those big dreams come true, you'll still have made progress improving life on this planet.

P.B.K.L. Agyirey-Kwakye's dad was a **forester**, so Agyirey-Kwakye learned a lot about trees as he was growing up. In 1990, when he was 14 years old, he decided to plant trees himself and share his knowledge. People told him the trees would take too long to grow and that the land was needed for vegetables. But Agyirey-Kwakye realized his neighbors in Kumikrom, Ghana, depended on firewood for fuel, and their crops would benefit from the trees' shade. He planted eucalyptus trees because he knew they'd grow quickly.

This environmental activist started the Youth Club for Nature Conservation. The group grew 2,000 eucalyptus seedlings, which they gave away to 14 farmers. The next year 290 more farmers signed up for the club's 10,000 trees. The program has provided renewable energy, conserved soil and taught people in Ghana about the environment.

FIGHTING FOR PEACE

Rigoberta Menchú Tum

(1959–)

TAKE ACTION

GIVE PEACE A CHANCE

Due to a mix-up, the obituary of Swedish businessman Alfred Nobel was published while he was still alive. The notice criticized him for inventing dynamite and other deadly explosives. Nobel wanted to change how people would remember him, so in 1895 he set up awards in the categories of chemistry, literature, medicine, peace and physics.

The Nobel Peace Prize is the world's top award for people who promote peace and work to put an end to war. Famous winners of the prize include activist Nelson Mandela, former United States president Barack Obama and nun and missionary Mother Teresa.

Rigoberta Menchú Tum is a woman of the K'iche' people, a Maya Indigenous group. As a girl growing up in Guatemala, she worked hard on a plantation, picking coffee beans. Her boss beat her if she didn't pick fast enough. He told her she was worthless.

Instead of accepting this unfair treatment, Menchú Tum became a human rights activist fighting for better working conditions for the Maya Peoples. She had little education, but she had big dreams of equal rights for her people.

Between 1960 and 1996, civil war engulfed Menchú Tum's country. She was born a year before the war started, and she saw how her family suffered throughout the conflict. Both of her brothers were murdered, her mother was tortured and killed, and her father was imprisoned a number of times before being killed.

Menchú Tum was exiled to Mexico in 1981 because of her opposition to the Guatemalan government. But she kept organizing strikes and demonstrations to stop the civil war. Menchú Tum cofounded the United Republic of Guatemalan Opposition. The government tried to silence her, but she kept telling her story.

Because of her hard work to end her country's war, Menchú Tum was awarded the Nobel Peace Prize in 1992. She was only 33 years old, making her the youngest winner of the prize. In 2006 Menchú Tum helped found the Nobel Women's Initiative, along with five other female Nobel Peace Prize winners. Their group works to improve women's rights around the world.

"I think the importance of doing activist work is precisely because it allows you to give back and to consider yourself not as a single individual."

—Angela Davis, Black rights activist

Menchú Tum (left) at a meeting of the Ibero-American Network of Agencies and Organizations against Discrimination (RIOOD) in 2016.

HARNESSING THE WIND

William Kamkwamba

(1987–)

RIGHTS AND REFUGEES

"I am most grateful for two things," said Yeonmi Park, "that I was born in North Korea and that I escaped from North Korea." Park's life under North Korea's dictatorship was so brutal that in 2007, when she was 13 years old, she and her mother escaped to China. They faced many hardships before they finally arrived in Seoul, South Korea.

Park gives speeches around the world about human rights and volunteers with activist groups. As a member of Liberty in North Korea (LiNK), she also works to protect other North Korean refugees.

William Kamkwamba loved school. But he grew up poor in a small rural town in Malawi, Africa, and his family couldn't afford to send him to high school. So Kamkwamba borrowed books from the local library. One book gave him the idea to build a windmill to provide power for his family's home.

It took Kamkwamba a few tries to create his windmill. His neighbors and family saw him working with a broken bicycle and an old tractor-fan blade and thought he was crazy. But Kamkwamba succeeded and went on to build a solar-powered water pump, drip irrigation system and more.

People started talking about Kamkwamba's accomplishments. Soon he was speaking at conferences around the world, and eventually he even went to university.

Kamkwamba knew that what had changed his life was education. So in 2008 he started the Moving

Windmills Project to help people living in rural Malawi. The group added solar panels to a local high school so kids could study at night. Kamkwamba's organization works with area leaders to come up with solutions for the problems they face.

For example, some young men in Kamkwamba's hometown of Wimbe were bored and getting into trouble. So the Moving Windmills Project sponsored a soccer team for them. The youths quickly learned discipline, and the team brought the community together to cheer for them. Soon local women were making money by selling snacks to the fans.

Kamkwamba dreams big to help make education available to people in Malawi and all over Africa.

This is one of the first windmills that William Kamkwamba built.

KEEPING KIDS SAFE

Song Kosal
(1984–)

Deadly Dangers

Nearly every hour, someone in the world is injured or killed by a landmine. No wonder Song Kosal wants to take her fight to ban them around the world.

Between 5,000 and 9,000 people are killed or injured by landmines and other explosive remnants of war each year, and most of them are civilians, not soldiers. More than half the victims are children—they're injured when they walk over the mines on their way to school.

More than 70 countries have been contaminated with landmines. As well as killing and maiming people and animals, they poison the soil around them, kill the roots of trees and release toxins into nearby streams.

"I don't want people to look at me and see only my missing leg. I am more than that. I am the same as you."

Song Kosal lost her right leg in 1990, when she was just five years old. She was working with her mom in a rice paddy on the Thailand-Cambodia border when she stepped on a hidden **landmine**.

Five years later the International Committee of the Red Cross came to Kosal's village, and she decided to join their campaign against landmines. She didn't want other kids to have a tragic accident like hers. Kosal went to Vienna to speak to a meeting of the United Nations, to ask them to ban landmines. She was so young that when she got up on the stage to speak, she forgot what she wanted to say!

Kosal continued to travel the world and dream big. In 1997 she was the first person to sign the Peoples Treaty in Canada's capital, Ottawa, to encourage all countries to ban landmines. A year later she started the campaign Youth Against War, with the slogan, "No more, no more war, no more landmine victims."

An ambassador for the International Campaign to Ban Landmines-Cluster Munition Coalition (ICBL-CMC), Kosal speaks at events around the world. "I can speak. I can be an example," she said. "I have to do something while I have the chance to."

"Every day," says Song Kosal, "I will do one thing to make peace grow like a flower."

So you want to be an accidental activist?

1. FIND YOUR PASSION: What change would you like to see in the world? What can you do to help make that change—in small ways or big? Follow your passion, and you can help change the world.

2. DON'T ACCEPT THINGS AS THEY ARE: If you see something unjust, think about what you can do to change it. It could be something in your community, your country or the world. Join others who believe as you do.

3. NOTICE WHAT'S NEEDED: The most important step in changing something is recognizing that it needs to be transformed.

4. JUST GET STARTED: Start small and don't be afraid to try! One tiny step in the right direction is better than nothing and can lead to big changes.

5. BE AN EXPERT: If you want to change something, learn all you can. Read. Observe. Discuss. Know your facts. Learn how to explain your position to others who don't have your knowledge.

6. STAY FOCUSED: Keep your goals in mind. Change doesn't happen overnight, so you have to be prepared to keep trying.

7. NETWORKING WORKS: Change is hard, but it's easier to work for it as a group. Find others who believe as you do. Discuss how you can make change together. Form larger groups.

8. BE FLEXIBLE: Always be alert to changing circumstances. Everything changes, and so will your approach. Observe and adjust based on how things change.

9. BE UNSTOPPABLE: Persistence makes things happen, so don't let bullies stop you. Be prepared to fail before you succeed.

10. DREAM BIG: Believe in yourself, and don't be afraid to set goals that seem difficult to meet. The world needs more dreamers!

GLOSSARY

acquitted—declared not guilty of a crime

activist—a person who works toward political or social change

advocate—to support and speak in favor of a group or movement (verb); someone who advocates (noun)

AIDS—abbreviation for *acquired immune deficiency syndrome*, a disease caused by the long-term presence of a virus that makes a person's body unable to protect itself from other diseases

apartheid—a policy in South Africa that divided people by race and discriminated against nonwhites

Asperger's syndrome—a mild autism spectrum disorder. People with it may have trouble with nonverbal communication and have poor social skills.

autism spectrum disorder (ASD)—a disorder in which people have difficulties in learning words and interacting with other people

boycott—refusal to buy items or have dealings with a place or organization in order to protest or create change

civil rights movement—an effort made by Black people and their supporters to eliminate segregation and gain equal rights for everyone, using such tactics as boycotts, marches and protests

civil war—a conflict that takes place between different groups in the same country

climate change—major changes in weather patterns (temperature, precipitation, etc.) brought about by human activity

depression—an illness that causes a person to feel persistent deep sadness, apathy, restlessness, irritability and/or many other emotions, usually for no apparent reason

diabetes—a disease caused by a person being unable to produce or use insulin, a chemical that helps people's bodies use sugar properly

discrimination—unjust treatment of people based on such characteristics as their sex, race or age

ecology—the science that studies how living things—plants, animals and people—interact with their environment

environment—all the plants, animals, buildings, etc. that surround a living thing and affect how it grows

exiled—being away or restricted from a certain place, often for political reasons

forester—a person who is an expert in the science of planting and caring for trees and forests

fossil fuels—nonrenewable fuels, such as coal, oil or natural gas, that come from the breakdown of the remains of plants or animals

free speech—the right to express information and ideas without government interference

hard-line—to deal with something in a firm way and refuse to change

hippie—a term from the 1960s for a young person who is unconventional in dress and behavior and believes in living a life based on peace and love

HIV—abbreviation for *human immuno-deficiency virus*, the virus that attacks the immune system and makes it harder for someone to fight off infections. Untreated, it can lead to AIDS.

Indigenous Peoples—the first or original inhabitants of an area, including First Nations people in Canada and the United States, and Aboriginal Australians

landmine—explosive device that's hidden underground and is set off by pressure, such as people walking or vehicles driving over it

landslide—a huge majority of votes for one political party

LGBTQ+—abbreviation for lesbian, gay, bisexual, transgender, queer and others

militant—someone who is combative and aggressive in support of a cause

Nazi—member of the National Socialist German Workers Party, which promoted dictatorial, racist policies and was led by Adolf Hitler

pandemic—a disease outbreak that occurs over a large geographic area, such as a whole country or the world, and affects a high proportion of the population

persecuted—harassed or punished unfairly, often for being perceived as different

plantation—a large farm or estate where crops such as cotton or rubber are grown for sale

poaching—the illegal capturing, hunting or killing of animals

polio—a disease that damages the nervous system and can cause paralysis (the full name is poliomyelitis)

prosecute—take legal action against a person

psychology—the science of behavior, mental processes and the mind

racism—the belief that one race is superior or inferior to another

residential schools—schools set up by the Canadian government that Indigenous children were forced to attend, where their Indigenous cultures and languages were stripped from them

savanna—a grassland containing scattered trees and drought-resistant undergrowth

Sharia law—an Islamic religious and traditional law that guides Muslims on daily life

slaughterhouse—a building where animals are killed and cut up for meat

thermonuclear—having to do with high-temperature nuclear reactions. The term is usually associated with weapons that use nuclear fusion to produce an enormous, destructive explosion.

think tank—a group of experts who provide ideas on various economic and political issues

United Nations (UN)—an organization made up of almost 200 countries that was started in 1945 to encourage nations to work for world peace

RESOURCES

PRINT

Brinkley, Douglas. *The Wilderness Warrior: Theodore Roosevelt and the Crusade for America.* New York: Harper, 2010.

Burns, Kate. *Gay Rights Activists.* Farmington Hills, MI: Lucent Books, 2005.

Chambers, Veronica. *Resist: 35 Profiles of Ordinary People Who Rose Up Against Tyranny and Injustice.* New York: HarperCollins, 2018.

Douglas, Marjory Stoneman. *The Everglades: River of Grass.* New York: Rhinehart and Co., 1947.

Drake, Jane, and Ann Love. *Yes You Can! Your Guide to Becoming an Activist.* Toronto: Tundra Books, 2010.

Dublin, Anne. *June Callwood: A Life of Action.* Toronto: Second Story Press, 2006.

Fern, Tracey. *Wild Horse Annie: Friend of the Mustangs.* New York: Farrar, Straus and Giroux, 2019.

Furstinger, Nancy. *Mercy: The Incredible Story of Henry Bergh, Founder of the ASPCA and Friend to Animals.* New York: Houghton Mifflin Harcourt, 2016.

Gleason, Carrie. *Environmental Activist.* St. Catharines, ON: Crabtree, 2009.

Goodall, Jane. *My Life with the Chimpanzees.* New York: Pocket Books, 1988.

Gore, Al. *An Inconvenient Truth: The Crisis of Global Warming.* New York: Viking, 2007.

Kamkwamba, William, and Bryan Mealer. *The Boy Who Harnessed the Wind: Young Readers Edition.* London: Puffin Books, 2016.

Larson, Jonah, and Jennifer Larson. *Hello, Crochet Friends! Making Art, Being Mindful, Giving Back: Do What Makes You Happy.* Milwaukee, WI: KWiL Publishing, 2019.

MacLeod, Elizabeth. *Meet Viola Desmond.* Toronto: Scholastic Canada, 2018.

McCreary, Michael. *Funny, You Don't Look Autistic: A Comedian's Guide to Life on the Spectrum.* Toronto: Annick Press, 2019.

Mirza, Sandrine. *People of Peace: 40 Inspiring Icons.* London: Wide Eyed Editions, 2018.

Park, Yeonmi. *In Order to Live: A North Korean Girl's Journey to Freedom.* London: Penguin Books, 2016.

Reed, Jennifer. *Elizabeth Bloomer: Child Labor Activist.* Mankato, MN: KidHaven Publishing, 2006.

Reich, Susanna. *Stand Up and Sing! Pete Seeger, Folk Music, and the Path to Justice.* New York: Bloomsbury, 2017.

Rose, Simon. *Indigenous Peoples in Politics.* Collingwood, ON: Beech Street Books, 2018.

Ruckel, Izidor, and Joan Bramsch. *Abandoned for Life: The Incredible Story of One Romanian Orphan Hidden from the World.* St. Louis, MO: Ruckel Intl, 2002.

Scandiffio, Laura. *People Who Said No: Courage Against Oppression.* Toronto: Annick Press, 2012.

Schlimm, John. *Stand Up!: 75 Young Activists Who Rock the World and How You Can, Too!* Orangevale, CA: Publishing Syndicate LLC, 2013.

Shoveller, Herb. *Ryan and Jimmy: And the Well in Africa that Brought Them Together.* Toronto: Kids Can Press, 2006.

Silvey, Anita. *Let Your Voice Be Heard: The Life and Times of Pete Seeger.* New York: Clarion Books, 2016.

Staley, Erin. *The Most Influential Female Activists.* Mankato, MN: Rosen Young Adult, 2018.

Sundem, Garth. *Real Kids, Real Stories, Real Change: Courageous Actions around the World.* Minneapolis: Free Spirit Publishing, 2010.

Thunberg, Greta. *No One Is Too Small to Make a Difference.* London: Penguin UK, 2019.

Warren, Sarah. *Dolores Huerta: A Hero to Migrant Workers.* Seattle: Amazon Publishing, 2012.

Webstad, Phyllis. *Phyllis's Orange Shirt.* Victoria, BC: Medicine Wheel Education, 2019.

Wing, Natasha. *When Jackie Saved Grand Central: The True Story of Jacqueline Kennedy's Fight for an American Icon.* New York: Houghton Mifflin Harcourt, 2017.

FILM

Morgan, Thomas, Francois Caillaud and Dan Chen. *Waiting for Mamu.* Charlotte, NC: Square Zero Films, 2013.

Nabors, Ben. *William and the Windmill.* New York: Group Theory, 2013.

ONLINE

Abisoye Ajayi Akinfolarin: cnn.com/2018/09/13/world/cnnheroes-abisoye-ajayi-akinfolarin-pearls-africa-foundation/index.html

Ai Weiwei: telegraph.co.uk/culture/art/art-features/9299885/Ai-Weiwei-The-police-can-be-very-tough-but-I-can-be-tougher-sometimes..html

Andrei Sakharov: nobelprize.org/prizes/peace/1975/sakharov/biographical

Bye Bye Plastic Bags: npr.org/sections/goatsandsoda/2019/01/26/688168838/how-teenage-sisters-pushed-bali-to-say-bye-bye-to-plastic-bags

The Climate Group: climateweeknyc.org/youth-are-governing-new-frontier-climate-activism

Craftivist Collective: craftivist-collective.com

Greenpeace: greenpeace.org/international/story/20165/5-young-activists-who-inspired-us-this-year

Gulalai Ismail: nytimes.com/2019/09/19/world/asia/gulalai-ismail-pakistan-activist.html

Jacinda Ardern: theguardian.com/world/2019/apr/06/jacinda-ardern-intuitive-courage-new-zealand

Joshua Tree: latimes.com/science/sciencenow/la-sci-col1-joshua-tree-minerva-hoyt-20190214-htmlstory.html

Joshua Wong: nytimes.com/2019/10/29/world/asia/joshua-wong-hong-kong-protests.html

Kailash Satyarthi: news.harvard.edu/gazette/story/2019/09/nobel-laureate-childrens-rights-activist-kailash-satyarthi-comes-to-harvard

Liz Christy: localeastvillage.com/2013/04/22/remebering-liz-christy-on-earth-day

Maziar Bahari: npr.org/2011/06/03/136862056/then-they-came-for-journalist-maziar-bahari

Michael McCreary: aspiecomic.com

Parkland students: theguardian.com/us-news/2019/feb/11/parkland-student-activists-march-for-our-lives-year-later-2019

Phyllis Jack Webstad: orangeshirtday.org

Puffin Patrol: cpawsnl.org/puffinpetrelpatrol

Pushpa Basnet: ecdcnepal.org

Ryan Hreljac: ryanswell.ca

Severn Cullis-Suzuki: vancouversun.com/news/local-news/before-greta-there-was-severn-the-b-c-girl-who-silenced-the-world

Tegan and Sara: teganandsara.com

INDEX

Page numbers in **bold** indicate an image caption.

PHOTO CREDITS

ACKNOWLEDGMENTS

Thanks so much to our wonderful editor, Kirstie Hudson, and designer Rachel Page. We also really appreciate the work of illustrator Jenn Playford and copyeditor Vivian Sinclair. Many thanks as well to Andrew Wooldridge and Ruth Linka of Orca Book Publishers, who believed in this book.

The world is constantly changing. No one knows what the future will hold, but activists like those we've profiled in our book continue to inspire us to do our part to make the world a better place.

Liz says: It's so inspiring to write about activists, especially the kids who are standing up and making changes. Thanks to Frieda for working with me on another book. It's always fun to investigate a new topic together! Many thanks to Laurie Dullaart and Brian Everett for their support. Thanks also to Janet Culliton, past president of Autism Ontario. Special thanks to John and Douglas, and love always to Paul.

Frieda says: Big thanks to my husband, Bill. I appreciate your insights and knowledge. And thanks, as always, to my wise and creative co-author Liz MacLeod. It's an honor to tell these true stories of courageous people who stand up and speak out to make the world a better place. We hope their stories will encourage others to change the world too.

ABOUT THE AUTHORS

Why do people do what they do? **Elizabeth MacLeod** loves finding that out and then sharing people's amazing stories with readers. Liz has written lots of books and won many prizes, including the Norma Fleck Award for Canadian Children's Non-Fiction, as well as Children's Choice awards across Canada. This is the fifth book Liz and Frieda have written together—their most recent is *How to Become an Accidental Genius.*

Frieda Wishinsky is the international award–winning author of over 70 books and a freelance editor. She writes picture books, chapter books, novels and nonfiction. Her books have been translated into many languages. Frieda believes that sharing stories is key to inspiring change in the world. She thinks that Elizabeth MacLeod is the best writing "partner" any author could have. Frieda lives in Toronto.

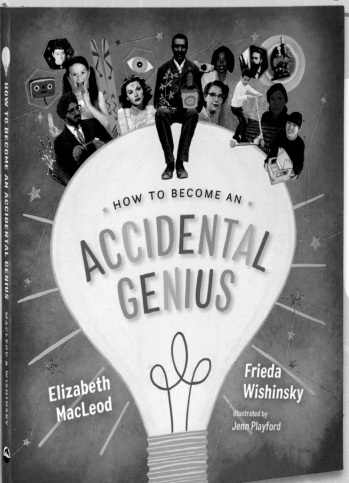